Wilfred Campbell

Lake Lyrics And Other Poems

Wilfred Campbell

Lake Lyrics And Other Poems

ISBN/EAN: 9783744714082

Printed in Europe, USA, Canada, Australia, Japan

Cover: Foto ©Thomas Meinert / pixelio.de

More available books at **www.hansebooks.com**

LAKE LYRICS AND OTHER POEMS BY WILLIAM WILFRED CAMPBELL.

ST. JOHN, N. B.
J. & A. McMILLAN.
1889.

Entered according to Act of Parliament of Canada, in the year 1889,
By WILLIAM WILFRED CAMPBELL.
In the Office of the Minister of Agriculture, at Ottawa.

CONTENTS.

PRELUDE: Vapor and Blue.

PART I.

	PAGE
To the Lakes,	13
A Lake Memory,	15
The Winter Lakes,	16
Keziah,	18
Morning on the Beach,	22
The Heart of the Lakes,	23
A Day of Mists,	25
Dawn in the Island Camp,	27
By Huron's Shore,	28
How Spring Came,	31
In the River Bay,	32
Lake Huron,	35
To the Blackberry,	36
Manitou,	39
Autumn's Chant,	41
The Flight of the Gulls,	44
A Lyric of Weariness,	46
August Evening on the Beach, Lake Huron,	48
Invocation to the Lakes,	51
A Lyric,	53
At the Landing,	54
Sunset, Lake Huron,	56
On the Ledge,	58
The Legend of Restless River,	60
The Legend of Dead Man's Lake,	65
Ode, To the Lakes,	69
Ode, To Thunder Cape,	72
Dan'l and Mat,	76
August Night on Georgian Bay,	79
The Tides of Dawn,	80
Crags,	81
Medwayosh,	82
At the River's Mouth,	83

PART II.

Snow,	87
Canadian Folksong,	89
To a Robin in November,	91
In the Study,	93
On Christmas Eve,	94
By the Fire,	95
Little Blue Eyes and Golden Hair,	96
Barberries,	98
The Passing Year,	99
A Winter's Night,	100
Old Voices,	102
February,	104
Midwinter Night's Dream,	106
On a March Morning,	107
Sunbeams,	109
Before the Dawn,	111
The Dewdrop,	112
Indian Summer,	113
To a Clump of Moss; Rododactulos,	114
The Meadow Spring,	115

PART III.

Lazarus,	119
The Hebrew Father's Prayer,	124
Ode, To Tennyson,	127
Ode, Canada to Great Britain,	132
Ode, To the Nineteenth Century,	136
Ode, To a Meadow Brook,	140
Alone,	142
Ballade of Two Riders,	144
A Lyric of Love,	148
The Phantoms of the Boughs on the Window,	151
Titan,	154
Isolation,	158
Infancy,	159
Knowledge,	160

PRELUDE.

VAPOR AND BLUE.

Domed with the azure of heaven,
  Floored with a pavement of pearl,
Clothed all about with a brightness
  Soft as the eyes of a girl,

Girt with a magical girdle,
  Rimmed with a vapor of rest —
These are the inland waters,
  These are the lakes of the west.

Voices of slumberous music,
  Spirits of mist and of flame,
Moonlit memories left here
  By gods who long ago came,

And vanishing left but an echo
  In silence of moon-dim caves,
Where haze-wrapt the August night slumbers,
  Or the wild heart of October raves.

Vapor and Blue.

Here where the jewels of nature
  Are set in the light of God's smile;
Far from the world's wild throbbing,
  I will stay me and rest me awhile.

And store in my heart old music,
  Melodies gathered and sung
By the genies of love and of beauty
  When the heart of the world was young.

PART I.

LAKE LYRICS.

TO THE LAKES.

BLUE, limpid, mighty, restless lakes,
  God's mirrors underneath the sky,
Low rimmed in woods and mists, where wakes,
  Through murk and moon, the marsh bird's cry.

Where ever on, through drive and drift,
  'Neath blue and grey, through hush and moan,
Your ceaseless waters ebb and lift
  Past shores of century-crumbling stone.

And under ever-changing skies,
  Swell, throb, and break on kindling beach;
Where fires of dawn responsive rise,
  In answer to your mystic speech.

Past lonely haunts of gull and loon,
  Past solitude of land-locked bays,
Whose bosoms rise to meet the moon,
  Beneath their silvered film of haze.

Where mists and fogs in ghostly bands,
  Vague, dim, moon-clothed in spectral light;
Drift in from far-off haunted lands,
  Across the silences of night.

A LAKE MEMORY.

THE lake comes throbbing in with voice of pain
   Across these flats, athwart the sunset's glow,
I see her face, I know her voice again,
   Her lips, her breath, O God, as long ago.

To live the sweet past over I would fain,
   As lives the day in the red sunset's fire,
That all these wild, wan marshlands now would stain,
   With the dawn's memories, loves and flushed desire.

I call her back across the vanished years,
   Nor vain — a white-armed phantom fills her place;
Its eyes the wind-blown sunset fires, its tears
   This rain of spray that blows about my face.

THE WINTER LAKES.

OUT in a world of death far to the northward lying,
Under the sun and the moon, under the dusk and the day;
Under the glimmer of stars and the purple of sunsets dying,
Wan and waste and white, stretch the great lakes away.

Never a bud of spring, never a laugh of summer,
Never a dream of love, never a song of bird;
But only the silence and white, the shores that grow chiller and dumber,
Wherever the ice winds sob, and the griefs of winter are heard.

Crags that are black and wet out of the gray lake looming,
Under the sunset's flush and the pallid, faint glimmer of dawn;

The Winter Lakes.

Shadowy, ghost-like shores, where midnight surfs are booming
Thunders of wintry woe over the spaces wan.

Lands that loom like specters, whited regions of winter,
Wastes of desolate woods, deserts of water and shore;
A world of winter and death, within these regions who enter,
Lost to summer and life, go to return no more.

Moons that glimmer above, waters that lie white under,
Miles and miles of lake far out under the night;
Foaming crests of waves, surfs that shoreward thunder,
Shadowy shapes that flee, haunting the spaces white.

Lonely hidden bays, moon-lit, ice-rimmed, winding,
Fringed by forests and crags, haunted by shadowy shores;
Hushed from the outward strife, where the mighty surf is grinding
Death and hate on the rocks, as sandward and landward it roars.

KEZIAH.

"Keziah! Keziah!" The blue lake is rocking,
Out over it's bosom the white gulls are flocking,
Far down in the west the dim islands are lying,
While through the hushed vapors the shores are
    replying:
"Keziah! Keziah!"

A vine-clambered cabin with blue skies that bound it,
Wild glamor of forest, lake, shoreland around it;
Far calling of birds, mists rising and falling,
While through the hushed silence a wierd voice is
    calling:
"Keziah! Keziah!"

She went down the shore-path her dark eyes were
    dreaming,
The sheen of her hair in the sunlight was gleaming,
The snow of her neck like the lake's snowy foaming,

And a man's promise met her down there in the
    gloaming:
"Keziah! Keziah!"

She went in her girlhood, her innocent sweetness,
She went in her trusting glad woman's completeness,
She went with a hope and returned with a sorrow,
A horrible dread of the coming to-morrow:
"Keziah! Keziah!"

The old woman moaneth, her meagre form swayeth,
"God's curse of all curses on him who betrayeth,"
O poor foolish girl-heart, dead, past our reproving,
God's hate on the base heart that played with her
    loving.
"Keziah! Keziah!"

O never, O never, while human hearts falter
Weak penitent prayers at the foot of God's altar,
Nor man's choking creeds nor heaven's dread
    ·thunder,

Can wipe out the curse from the lives that sleep
    under.
"Keziah! Keziah!"

The girl like a flower caught late in life's snowing,
Too full of love's summer for October's blowing,
Died quick in her shame, the mother her sadness,
Wore out into bitterness, sorrow, then madness.
"Keziah! Keziah!"

Years after she'd sit by the hut door at even,
When vapors were soft over lake shore and heaven,
And dream in her madness a girl-figure coming,
With youth's dreamy beauty in out of the gloaming.
"Keziah! Keziah!"

Dead, gone, these long years by the hut-side she's
    sleeping,
Where over it's dead walls the red vines are
    creeping,
But the fisher-folk say that at summer eves falling,

In out of the stillness they hear a voice calling:
"Keziah! Keziah!"

And over the lake with its glamor of vapors,
Through which the faint stars soon will glimmer
    like tapers,
From the dim islands lit with the purpled day's
    dying,
Like a far, caverned echo a faint voice replying:
"Keziah! Keziah!"

MORNING ON THE BEACH.
(Lake Huron, June.)

SEE the night is beginning to fail,
The stars have lost half of their glow;
As though all the flowers in a garden did pale,
When a rose is beginning to blow.

And the breezes that herald the dawn,
Blown round from the caverns of day;
Lift the film of dark from the heavens bare lawn,
Cool and sweet as they come up this way.

And this mighty swayed bough of the lake
Rocks cool where the morning hath smiled;
While the dim, misty dome of the world scarce awake
Blushes rose, like the cheek of a child.

THE HEART OF THE LAKES.

THERE are crags that loom like spectres
  Half under the sun and the mist;
There are beaches that gleam and glisten,
There are ears that open to listen,
  And lips held up to be kissed.

There are miles and miles of waters
  That throb like a woman's breast,
With a glad harmonious motion
  Like happiness caught at rest,
As if a heart beat under
  In love with its own glad rest;
Beating and beating forever,
  Outward to east and to west.

There are forests that kneel forever,
  Robed in the dreamiest haze
That God sends down in the summer

To mantle the gold of its days,
Kneeling and leaning forever
In winding and sinuous bays.

There are birds that like smoke drift over,
With a strange and bodeful cry,
Into the dream and the distance
Of the marshes that southward lie,
With their lonely lagoons and rivers,
Far under the reeling sky.

A DAY OF MISTS.

The crags and the low shores kneel
Like ghosts, in the fogs that reel,
And glide, and shiver, and feel
  For the shores with their shadowy hands.
Earth and heaven are grey;
The worlds of waters are grey,
And out in the fog-haunted day
  A spectre — the lighthouse — stands.

And far from some caverned shore,
There cometh the distant roar
  Of the lake-surf's beat and din;
While wraith-like over the land,
From low white isles of sand
Of far off Michigan,
  The fogs come drifting in.

I stand in the shrouded day,
But my heart is far away

With a grave in a lonely bay,
  Where the crags like eaglets cling;
And under the drive and drift
Of the vapors that sometime lift,
And loom, and lower, and shift,
  The lake-birds scream and sing.

DAWN IN THE ISLAND CAMP.

RED in the mists of the morning,
   Angry, colored with fire,
Beats the great lake in its beauty,
   Rocks the wild lake in its ire.

Tossing from headland to headland,
   Tipped with the glories of dawn,
With gleaming, wide reaches of beaches,
   That stretch out far, wind-swept and wan.

Behind, the wild tangle of island,
   Swept and drenched by the gales of the night;
In front, lone stretches of water
   Flame-bathed by the incoming light:

Dim the dark reels and dips under,
   Night wavers and ceases to be;
As God sends the manifold mystery
   Of the morning and lake round to me.

BY HURON'S SHORE.

HERE amid the smoke of cities,
Where far heaven never pities
Earth, and kisses her with flowers;
Through the weary, sunless hours,
  How I long for Huron's shore:
How I long for Huron's beaches,
Where the wind-swept, shining reaches
  Wind in mists and are no more.

How I long for sky and water,
Where is never dearth of thought, or
Lack of love for heaven's blue;
Where all nature loveth true,
  By the sky-rimmed, shining floor,
By the black, wet caverned ledges,
By the sands where windy sedge is
  Kissed by Huron evermore.

By Huron's Shore.

How I long for dawns in-blowing,
For the day-bloom, ruddier growing,
Into morning's perfect flower;
Watched in sweet, wind rustled hour,
   Spirit-wrapt, by Huron's shore,
Where the stars die out like tapers,
And the islands, clad in vapors,
   Rise at heaven's opened door.

Where the great lake's shining bosom
Rocks like some blue, petalled blossom,
Blossomed 'mid the night's sweet care,
Wind-shook in the morning air;
   How I long for Huron's shore,
Just to watch the dawns uprising,
Over wave and crag, surprising
   Earth to life and love once more.

How I long for suns, low-setting,
Through the even's vaulted fretting,
Till the stars resumed their marches
Past the sky's great vaulted arches,

Over earth's cathedral floor.
Then it was we stood together,
She and I, while God's glad weather
Haze-wrapt heaven, wave and shore.

O to stand by Huron's beaches,
By those glorious, sun-bathed reaches,
In that dream of light and mist,
Earth-embraced and heaven-kissed,
Just to stand by Huron's shore,
Just to know the old thoughts banished,
Just to dream a face long vanished, —
Vanished, dead, to come no more.

HOW SPRING CAME.
(To the Lake Region.)

No passionate cry came over the desolate places,
    No answering call from iron-bound land to land;
But dawns and sunsets fell on mute, dead faces,
    And noon and night, death crept from strand to strand.

'Till love breathed out across the wasted reaches,
    And dipped in rosy dawns from desolate deeps;
And woke with mystic songs the sullen beaches,
    And flamed to life the pale, mute, death-like sleeps.

Then the warm south, with amorous breath inblowing,
    Breathed soft o'er breast of wrinkled lake and mere;
And faces white from scorn of the north's snowing,
    Now rosier grew to greet the kindling year.

IN THE RIVER BAY.

ALONE I pause in morning dream
Upon the border of the stream,
Where all the summer melts away,
In mists of wood and sky and bay;
And voices of the morning wake
In whispers from the distant lake.
With dews down fallen from the night,
The alders scintilate in light.
Reflected in the river pool,
The woods bend restful, sweet and cool.
And hidden in their heart away,
A thrush sends forth his roundelay,
Echo'd in the airs above,
Filling all heaven and earth with love.

Above me in the darkling wood,
Through dusks of morning solitude,
Drifting in many a watery moon,
The river chants a sleepy tune.

In the River Bay.

Far out in front, in shining curves,
Where, sun-cuirassed, his soft tide swerves,
And all the dreams of morning brood,
His shores wind, mirroring in his flood.

With half-shut eyes I muse and see
This morning picture dreamily.
Then throbbeth up within my heart
(Which seemeth nature's counterpart),
A wish to stay and dream for aye,
The morning by this river-bay,
To stay forever and forget
The new desire and old regret,
The doubt, the sorrow, and the curse,
The passions that our spirits nurse;
To never dream in morning's fires
The ghosts of vanished, dead desires;
To never read in kindling skies
The sadness of reproachful eyes:
Refined, removed of all earth's dross,
It's strife, its sorrow, and its loss,

To be a little child for aye,
Mist-cradled in this river-bay.

The dream is sweet but all too soon,
Is lost it's vision, hushed it's rune;
For up along the river-wall
I hear my comrades gaily call:
The dream is broken, life reclaims,
To darker fancies, sterner aims.
I leave my restful river-bay,
And worldward once more wend my way.

LAKE HURON.
(October.)

MILES and miles of lake and forest,
    Miles and miles of sky and mist,
Marsh and shoreland where the rushes
    Rustle, wind and water kissed;
Where the lake's great face is driving,
    Driving, drifting into mist.

Miles and miles of crimson glories,
    Autumn's wondrous fires ablaze;
Miles of shoreland red and golden,
    Drifting into dream and haze;
Dreaming where the woods and vapors,
    Melt in myriad misty ways.

Miles and miles of lake and forest,
    Miles and miles of sky and mist,
Wild birds calling where the rushes
    Rustle, wind and water kissed;
Where the lake's great face is driving,
    Driving, drifting into mist.

TO THE BLACKBERRY.

I FIND thee by the country side,
  With angry mailèd thorn;
When first with dreamy woods and skies
  The summer time is born.

By every fence and woodland path
  Thy milk-white blossom blows;
In lonely haunts of mist and dream,
  The summer airs enclose.

And when the freighted August days
  Far into Autumn lean;
Sweet, luscious, on the laden branch,
  Thy ripened fruit is seen.

Dark gypsy of the glowing year,
  Child of the sun and rain,
While dreaming by thy tangled path,
  There comes to me again,

To the Blackberry.

The memory of a happy boy,
   Barefooted, freed from school,
Who plucked your rich lip-staining fruit,
   By road-ways green and cool.

And tossed in glee his ragged cap,
   With laughter to the sky;
Oblivious in the glow of youth,
   How the mad world went by;

Nor cared in realms of summer time,
   By haunts of bough and vine,
If Nicholas lost the Volga,
   Or Bismark held the Rhine.

O time when shade with sun was blent,
   So like an April shower;
Life has its flower and thorn and fruit,
   But thou wert all its flower.

When every day Nepenthe lent,
   To drown its deepest sorrow,

To the Blackberry.

And evening skies but prophesied
A glorious skied to-morrow.

O, long gone days of sunlit youth,
I'd live through years of pain,
Once more life's fate of thorn and fruit
To dream your flower again.

MANITOU.
(The Island sacred to the Memory of Manitou in Lake Huron.)

GIRDLED by Huron's throbbing and thunder,
    Out on the drift and lift of its blue;
Walled by mists from the world asunder,
Far from all hate and passion and wonder,
    Lieth the isle of the Manitou.

Here, where the surfs of the great lake trample,
    Thundering time-worn caverns through,
Beating on rock-coasts aged and ample;
Reareth the Manitou's mist-walled temple,
    Floored with forest and roofed with blue.

Gray crag-battlements, seared and broken,
    Keep these passes for ages to come;
Never a watchword here is spoken,
Never a single sign or token,
    From hands that are motionless, lips that are dumb.

Only the Sun-god rideth over,
  Marking the seasons with track of flame;
Only the wild-fowl float and hover —
Flocks of clouds whose white wings cover
  Spaces on spaces without a name.

Year by year the ages onward
  Drift, but it lieth out here alone;
Earthward the mists and the earth-mists sunward,
Starward the days, and the nights blown dawnward,
  Whisper the forests, the beaches make moan.

Far from the world and its passions fleeting,
  'Neath quiet of noon-day and stillness of star,
Shore unto shore each sendeth greeting;
Where the only woe is the surf's wild beating
  That throbs from the maddened lake afar.

AUTUMN'S CHANT.

FROM the far-off, mighty rivers,
Drifting, shifting, glad-life givers,
　　Throbbing, pulsing, to the lakes;
From the far-off, blue-peaked mountains,
From the forest-girdled fountains,
　　Where the sunlight leaps and shakes;
　　From the spaces wild and dreary,
　　From the cornlands far and near,
　　Comes the Autumn's miserere,
　　Comes the death song of the year.

Comes the music of far voices,
Where the season rich, rejoices,
　　Half reluctant now to go:—
Over lands of dreams and vapors,
Where wild hosts with half burnt tapers
　　Light her to the days of snow;
　　Over fields all yellow, burning

With their store of ruddy heat,
Under forests, ripe and turning
Red and gold beneath her feet.

From the golden, undulating
Wheat fields, where the glad, pulsating
  Gleam of mowers, moves along —
Through the day so rich and heavy,
Belled with bees a pollened bevy,
  Jargoning their honied song ;
  Comes the music of far voices
  Dying, swelling, here to me ;
  Thuswise all the earth rejoices
  At the year's maturity.

From far, northern lakes a clanging
Note of wild-geese, where low-hanging
  Mists drift over marshes bleak ;
In a world of smoke and shadow,
Where, far over wild lake-meadow,
  Sunsets burn on field and creek ;
  Comes with all the lakes far moaning

Autumn's Chant.

On some bare coast bleak and drear,
Voices wild and sweet intoning
Music of the dying year.

From the forest rich and gleaming,
Where the old year sitteth dreaming
  By a smoky, curling brook;
Hour by hour new wonders learning
Like to one who sitteth turning
  Pages of some magic book:
  Sound of nuts and dead leaves falling,
  Lonely note of crows and jays,
  Lowing herd and squirrel calling,
  Chanteth sweet of Autumn days.

THE FLIGHT OF THE GULLS.

OUT over the spaces,
The sunny, blue places,
  Of water and sky;
Where day on day merges
  In nights that reel by;
Through calms and through surges,
Through stormings and lulls,
O, follow,
      Follow,
The flight of the gulls.

With wheeling and reeling,
With skimming and stealing,
  We wing with the wind,
Out over the heaving
Of gray waters, leaving
  The lands far behind
And dipping ships' hulls.
O, follow,
      Follow,
The flight of the gulls.

The Flight of the Gulls.

Up over the thunder
Of reefs that lie under,
  And dead sailors' graves;
Like snowflakes in summer,
Like blossoms in winter,
  We float on the waves,
And the shore-tide that pulls.
O, follow,
      Follow,
The flight of the gulls.

Would you know the wild vastness
Of the lakes in their fastness,
  Their heaven's blue span;
Then come to this region,
  From the dwellings of man.
Leave the life-care behind you,
That nature annuls,
And follow,
      Follow,
The flight of the gulls.

A LYRIC OF WEARINESS.

SWEETER to listen thy singing
Than wearisome babble of men;
  To hearken down close to thy singing,
  Thy bells so tumultuous, ringing,
On marshlands and wind-tangled fen.
  Full-wearied, to drink in and listen
  The ripple of waters that glisten,
  Forgetting the babble of men.

  Forgetting the gibe and the sneering;
The pettiness, rancor and fray
  Of a world whose birth and appearing,
  Whose jealousies, struggles, and jeering,
And curses are but for a day.
  Close-brother to bud and to blossom
  Low-cradled in summer's warm bosom,
  I drink the sweet peace of the day.

A Lyric of Weariness.

The mad world may buckle its armor,
May gird itself strong to the strife;
  It may heat its wierd furnaces warmer,
  Yea seven times seven still warmer,
Till the white flame slays like a knife:
  But dead to it's curse and ambition,
  I listen the waves' soft petition,
And rest me apart from the strife.

  O brothers, what matter, what reason,
To struggle a few weary hours?
  Better be one of the bees in
  The blossoms one sweet little seasón,
To gather the honey of flowers.
  To gather the sunshine and sweetness,
  And round out life's little completeness,
Passing away with the hours.

AUGUST EVENING ON THE BEACH, LAKE HURON.

A LURID flush of sunset sky,
   An angry sketch of gleaming lake,
I will remember till I die
The sound, of pines that sob and sigh,
   Of waves upon the beach that break.

'Twas years ago, and yet it seems,
   O love, but only yesterday
We stood in holy sunset dreams,
While all the day's diaphonous gleams
   Sobbed into silence bleak and gray.

We scarcely knew, but our two souls
   Like night and day rushed into one;
The stars came out in gleaming shoals:
While, like a far-off bell that tolls,
   Came voices from the wave-dipped sun.

August Evening on the Beach, Lake Huron.

We scarcely knew, but hand in hand,
    With subtle sense, was closer pressed;
As we two walked in that old land
Forever new, whose shining strand
    Goes gleaming round the world's great breast.

What was it sweet our spirits spoke?
    No outward sound of voice was heard.
But was it bird or angel broke
The silence, till a dream voice woke
    And all the night was music-stirred?

What was it, love, did mantle us,
    Such fire of incense filled our eyes?
The moon-light was not ever thus:
Such star-born music rained on us,
    We grew so glad and wonder-wise.

But this, O love, was long ago,
    Although it seems but yesterday
The moon rose in her silver glow,
As she will rise on nights of woe,
    On hands uplift, on hearts that pray.

August Evening on the Beach, Lake Huron.

A lurid flush of sunset sky,
  An angry sketch of gleaming lake;
I will remember till I die,
The sound of pines that sob and sigh,
  Of waves upon the beach that break.

INVOCATION TO THE LAKES.

I LOVE thee, lakes, and all thy glorious world,
    Blue, wrinkled, mist-encircled 'neath the sky.
And far unto thy realm of waves impearled
    My heart, bird-like, doth fly.

Thou art to me as love to lover sad,
    As sun to flower, as husband unto wife;
I think of thee and all the hours are glad,
    And dead are pain and strife.

Thou comest to me as cooling draught to one,
    Hot parched and faint with unassuagéd thirst;
My spirit tranced within thy air and sun
    Forgets the world is cursed.

Thou knowest nor hate, nor death, nor sin, nor pain,
    Nor woeful partings, bitterness and tears;
But only days that sleep to wake again,
    Across thy golden years.

Within thy dreamy borders nought takes shape
  Of weird ambition, sorrow at the heart's core:
Thou holdest only love of cape for cape,
  Of murmurous shore for shore.

From sky and wave I drink thy nectared draught,
  From jewelled brim that stars of heaven span:
When, lo, 'tis love for God my heart hath quaffed,
  And sympathy for man.

A LYRIC.

I would bring you a song, O lakes:
  A song of delight and desire;
A song of the spring that wakes,
Of the warm red light that shakes
  Far over your white ice-pyre.

I would breathe you a song, O lakes;
  A song of the love that thrills
The heart of the year, and breaks
The fetters of winter, and slakes
  The thirst of the season in rills.

I would breathe you a song, O lakes;
  And the bountiful answer you give,
And the love and music it wakes,
Trances my spirit and makes
  Me thankful to God that I live.

AT THE LANDING.

I CANNOT hear you owning
  Your mighty love for me;
For all the lakes far moaning,
For all the waves' intoning,
  Brings back a love to me:
  A love that might not be.

The white-winged gulls were flying
  Across the purple light;
Where all our day was dying
On lands dim sunk and lying
  Far-off where loomed the night;
  And dusk hours wheeled their flight.

He stood where you are standing,
  The west enshrined his brow;
Across the white, scarred landing,
Wave after wave was stranding,

Then back with moan and sough;
He spoke as you spoke now.

He told what you are telling,
  While a sweet, undreamed of pain
Up in my heart was welling;
He told the tale whose telling
  Can ne'er be told again:
  O love, but all in vain!

Forgive, this sudden feeling,
  This strange outburst of woe,
This woman-weakness stealing
O'er me, as though days, reeling,
  Brought back the long ago;
  For love remembers so.

I could not have you speaking
  Your love, like his, to me;
While shores white moan were making,
And all my heart was breaking,
  For a love that could not be;
  O, love, it might not be!

SUNSET, LAKE HURON.
(September.)

THE sunbeams fall in golden flakes,
　　Like snow-banks flamed the clouds are furled ;
The soft light shakes
On wave that breaks
　　On wave, far round the gleaming world.

Great brown, bare rocks, wet, purple dyed,
　　By sunsets beams hedge in this realm
Of sky and wide,
Bleak sweep of tide,
　　Grey, tossed, scarce-plowed by keel or helm.

The east looms dark, the red day dips
　　Down under gleaming rock and wave,
In hushed eclipse,
While grey night slips
　　The cerements of her shrouded grave.

Sunset, Lake Huron.

And buildeth up her arches dark,
  From ruins of the dim dead day,
Till earth may mark
Each luminous spark,
  Of stars that far in heaven stray.

And weaveth with her phantom hands
  (Blind, dumb, save for the moon's white wreath,
And rude wind bands
From Eblis lands)
  A shroud for the great lake beneath;

That beats and moans, a prisoned thing,
  Rock-manacled beneath the night;
And tells each shore,
Forever more
  Its sorrow in the pallid light.

ON THE LEDGE.

I LIE out here on a ledge with the surf on the rocks
    below me,
The hazy sunlight above and the whispering forest
    behind ;
I lie and listen, O lake, to the legends and songs you
    throw me,
Out of the murmurous moods of your multitudinous
    mind.

I lie and listen a sound like voices of distant thunder,
The roar and throb of your life in your rock wall's
    mighty cells;
Then after a softer voice that comes from the beaches
    under,
A chiming of waves on rocks, a laughter of silver bells.

A glimmer of bird-like boats, that loom from the far
    horizon ;

That scud and tack and dip under the gray and the
 blue;
A single gull that floats and skims the waters, and
 flies on
Till she is lost like a dream, in the haze of the distance,
 too.

A steamer that rises a smoke, then after a tall, dark
 funnel,
That moves like a shadow across your water and sky's
 gray edge;
A dull, hard beat of a wave that diggeth himself a
 tunnel,
Down in the crevices dark under my limestone ledge.

And here I lie on my ledge, and listen the songs you
 sing me,
Songs of vapor and blue, songs of island and shore;
And strange and glad are the hopes and sweet are the
 thoughts you bring me,
Out of the throbbing depths and wells of your heart's
 great store.

THE LEGEND OF RESTLESS RIVER.

INTO the vague unrest
Of Huron's mighty breast,
   Runneth the Restless River.
Into the north and west,
Out of the forest's rest
   Its face is set forever.

Moons wane through spaces white,
As marsh-birds wheel their flight,
As dawns reel into night,
   And souls from souls dissever;
But over the sands to the bay,
Past the forests that pray,
   The river it runneth forever.

It was a curse and worse,
   A curse on the Restless River;
Moons and moons ago,

Before the ages of snow,
And ice, and rains that shiver,
 Came the curse of the Restless River.

What was this terrible curse?
Never in tale or verse,
Did singer or chief rehearse;
 Warrior sang it never;
But only the Manitou,
Who knoweth all things, knew,
The moons and ages through,
 The secret of Restless River.

Where other streams might sleep,
In eddies cool and deep,
Beneath where cascades leap
 In sunny snowy surges;
With never a dreaming place,
With never a breathing space,
In one wild tortuous race,
 Its maddened tide it urges.

Why this horrible dread,
This fear of the midnight dead,
When the stars peer overhead,
   Out of lone spaces winging?
Men said that the stars and moon
At the silence of midnight noon,
   Never mirrored themselves in its singing.

That its song was only a moan;
For a sin it could never atone,
Of all earth's waters alone,
   It runs in the darkness forever;
And that never the song of bird,
Save only in sadness, is heard
   On the shores of the Restless River.

Men say, at noon of day,
In thickets far away,
Where skies are dim and gray,
   And birches stir and shiver,
That out of the gloomy air,

A voice goes up in prayer,
  From the shores of the Restless River.

Whatever its sin hath been,
Its shores are just as green,
And over it kindly lean
  Great forests heavenward growing;
And its waters are just as sweet,
And its tides more strong and fleet
  Than any river flowing.

But for all its outward mirth
And the glow that spans its girth,
Its voices from air and earth,
  Its walls of leaves that quiver;
Men say an awful curse
And dread as death, and worse,
  Hangs over the Restless River.

And the dreamy Indian girl,
As she sees its waters curl,
In many a silver whirl,

Hath pity on Restless River,
For she knows that long ago,
Its tides that once were slow,
By reason of some dread woe,
   Went suddenly swift forever;
That a dread and unknown curse,
For a sin, or something worse,
   Was laid on the Restless River.

THE LEGEND OF DEAD MAN'S LAKE.*

EVER a gray haze waketh the morn,
    In a region that all forsake,
And the noons they follow the desolate noons,
    On the shores of the Dead Man's Lake.

'Tis a world of forest all withered and bleak,
    Where never a leaf doth grow;
But a grey mist broods over water and woods,
    Twixt heaven and earth below;
And never a sound in all the world round,
    But the desolate call of a crow.

---

* Dead Man's Lake, a lonely sheet of water that lies in a desolate region of the Indian Peninsula, between Lake Huron and Georgian Bay. It is situated in a forest of dead pines and hemlocks, blighted by bush fires long before the memory of any living man, and this adds materially to the desolation of an already dreary region of swamp and rock. The Indians have a legend that a chief was treacherously murdered on this lake, and that his body still lies with upturned face at the bottom. Hence its name and the dread curse they believe hangs over the vicinity, which they always shun. .

And there in a mist, by clammy winds kissed,
  Where never a creature is seen,
All fringed in with weeds and dank marsh reeds
  The lake it lieth between.

The golden summers they go and they come;
  The seasons they wake and they sleep;
The partridge drum, and the wild bees' hum,
  Are heard over meadow and deep;
But never the golden summers that come,
  Or the seasons that sleep and wake,
Can waken the rest that broods on the breast
  Of the desolate Dead Man's Lake.

There is never a ray of the sun by day,
  But ever that horrible haze,
That hangs like a shroud or the ghost of a cloud
  All about the dread hush of its days:
And ever the moon at her midnight noon,
  Half a cloak doth her cloud-veil make,
As she peers with a pallid and startled look
  In the bosom of Dead Man's Lake.

And ever, 'tis said, that she seeth a dread,
    White face of a long-dead man,
That floateth down there, with the weeds in its hair,
    And a look so fixed and wan;
Like the ghost of a hate, that lieth in wait,
    Through the years that it longeth to span.

And ever at midnight, white and drear,
    When the dim moon sheddeth her light,
Will the startled deer, as they speed by here,
    Slacken their phantom-like flight;
And into the shade that the forest hath made,
    A wider circle they take;
For they dread lest their tread wake the sleep of the dead
    In the bosom of Dead Man's Lake.

And as long as it lies with that prayer in its eyes,
    And that curse on its white-sealed lips,
Will the lake lie wan, and the years drift on,
    In their horrible, hushed eclipse,

The Legend of Dead Man's Lake.

Will the lake lie under the strange mute wonder
    Of the moon as she pallidly dips;

Will the song of the bird there never be heard,
    Nor the music of wind-swept tree,
But only the dread of the skies overhead,
    That the mists will never set free,
From the terrible spell that there ever will dwell
    As long as the ages be.

And there it lies and holdeth the skies,
    In a trance they never can break,
While the years, they follow the desolate years,
    On the shores of the Dead Man's Lake.

ODE.

TO THE LAKES.
(In June.)

O MAGIC region of blue waters throbbing,
    O blown wave-garden, 'neath the north world's span;
Wild paradise, girt in by crag-walls, robbing
    All earth of beauty since the world began;
I dream again your voice of beaches sobbing
    And crave a boon more sweet than gift of man;—

Once more in the ripe heart of golden summer,
    To drift upon your blue pearled wimpling breast;
To watch God's dawn, bud, bloom, a flushed incomer,
    To see him die with flames in thy hushed west;
To even know the entranced silence dumber,
    Because of heart awe-hushed and lips love-pressed.

To watch the dimmed day deepen into even,
    The flush of sunset melt in pallid gold;

To the Lakes.

While the pale planets blossom out in heaven ;
  To feel the under silence trance and hold
The night's great heartbeats ; soul-washed, nature-shriven,
  To feel the mantle of silence fold on fold.

To know the horologe of nature timing
  The dawning or the golden heart of noon,
To hear in spirit magic bells set chiming
  On silver continents of the rising moon ;
To read in sky, wave, wood, God's poet rhyming
  In mystic rhythm nature's eternal rune.

And so forget the sorrow and the glory,
  The passion and the pain that men call life;
To let the past go like a long-told story,
  The long-forgotten and the long-dead strife ;
But just to drift here while the years grow hoary,
  Dead to earth's living with all it's anguish rife.

And know no voice save that of beaches chanting,
  No eye save June's own glorious dome of blue;

And so be dead to all the strife and canting,
   The violence of souls that were untrue;
And only know one love, the mighty panting
   Of your great heart that throbs your being through.

ODE.

TO THUNDER CAPE.*

STORM-BEATEN cliff, thou mighty cape of thunder;
Rock-Titan of the north, whose feet the waves beat under;
Cloud-reared, mist-veiled, to all the world a wonder,
Shut out in thy wild solitude asunder,
  O Thunder Cape, thou mighty cape of storms.

About thy base, like wo that naught assuages,
Throughout the years the wild lake raves and rages;
One after one, time closes up weird pages;
But firm thou standest, unchanged, through the ages,
  O Thunder Cape, thou awful cape of storms.

Upon thy ragged front, the storm's black anger,
Like eagle clings, amid the elements' clangor:

---

* Thunder Cape, an immense cliff of basaltic rock, thirteen hundred feet high, guards the entrance to Thunder Bay, Lake Superior.

To Thunder Cape.

About thee feels the lake's soft sensuous languor;
But dead alike to loving and to anger,
  Thou towerest bleak, O mighty cape of storms.

Year in, year out, the summer rain's soft beating,
Thy front hath known, the winter's snow and sleeting;
But unto each thou givest contemptuous greeting.
These hurt thee not through seasons fast and fleeting;
  O proud, imperious, rock-ribbed cape of storms.

In August nights, when on thy under beaches,
The lake to caverns time-wierd legend teaches;
And moon-pearled waves to shadowed shores send speeches,
Far into heaven, thine awful darkness reaches,
  O'ershadowing night; thou ghostly cape of storms.

In wild October, when the lake is booming
It's madness at thee, and the north is dooming
The season to fiercest hate, still unconsuming,
Over the strife, thine awful front is looming;
  Like death in life, thou awful cape of storms.

To Thunder Cape.

Across thy rest the wild bee's noonday humming,
And sound of martial hosts to battle drumming,
Are one to thee — no date knows thine incoming;
The earliest years belong to thy life's summing,
  O ancient rock, thou aged cape of storms.

O thou so old, within thy sage discerning,
What sorrows, hates, what dead past loves still-burning,
Couldst thou relate, thine ancient pages turning;
O thou, who seemest ever new lores learning,
  O unforgetting, wondrous cape of storms.

O tell me what wild past lies here enchanted:
What borders thou dost guard, what regions haunted?
What type of man a little era flaunted,
Then passed and slept? O tell me thou undaunted,
  Thou aged as eld, O mighty cape of storms.

O speak, if thou canst speak, what cities sleeping?
What busy streets? what laughing and what weeping?
What vanished deeds and hopes like dust upheaping,
Hast thou long held within thy silent keeping?
  O wise old cape, thou rugged cape of storms.

These all have passed, as all that's living passes;
Our thoughts they wither as the centuries' grasses,
That bloom and rot in bleak, wild lake morasses:
But still thou loomest where Superior glasses
   Himself in surge and sleep, O cape of storms.

And thou wilt stay when we and all our dreaming
Lie low in dust. The age's last moon-beaming
Will shed on thy wild front it's final gleaming;
For last of all that's real and all that's seeming,
   Thou still wilt linger, mighty cape of storms.

DAN'L AND MAT.

Haint never heard of the Renshaws?
  Two brothers, Dan'l and Mat,
Lived down the shores of Huron,
  On an island they called Big Hat;
Where the waves run high'rn mountains,
  And the beaches is foggy and flat.

Dan'l was tall and strappin',
  But Mat he was scraggy and lean:
Allus half-dead with the agy,
  Caused by the liver or spleen.
But the 'fection betwixt them two brothers
  Was a tarnal fine sight ter be seen.

They war'nt never properly edicated,
  Least not in the reg'lar way
Of colleges, churches, and meetins;

But I bet they was a 'spletive long way
Ahead in livin' and actin'
Of mos'n of those who pray.

Histories, lies you might call them,
　But such stories them fellers could tell —
Beat old Robertson Cruiser,
　And 'Rabian nights as well;
An all of the gospellest truth, sir,
　As them as heerd em could tell.

Night after night, down at Masons',
　As drinkin an smokin we sat;
'Magination, not lies, sir,
　For no un ud contradict flat,
When Mat ud coroborate Dan'l,
　An Dan'l ud swear by Mat.

An once when a half fool feller,
　Stood up an said t'was all rot;
Ef it had'nt a bin fer Dan'l
　(A tarnation fighter when hot),

I believe as the crowd in the barroom
   Would a murdered that chap on the spot.

Dead, yes, gone these years, sir,
   Out fishin and caught in a squall;
Each tried ter resky the other,
   But the lake as, is hard on us all,
Washed their bodies ashore next mornin,
   High and dry up, and that's all.

But ef lovin yer brother means heaven,
   They've got it an mor'n that,
For you'll find them away down the shore there,
   On the island that's called Big Hat;
And Mat he lies close up to Dan'l,
   An Dan'l he's sleepin by Mat.

AUGUST NIGHT, ON GEORGIAN BAY.

THE day dreams out, the night is brooding in,
Across this world of vapor, wood, and wave.
Things blur and dim. Cool silvery ripples lave
   The sands and rustling reed-beds. Now begin
   Night's dreamy choruses, the murmurous din
Of sleepy voices. Tremulous, one by one,
The stars blink in. The dusk drives out the sun;
   And all the world the hosts of darkness win.

Anon, through mists, the harvest moon will come,
   With breathing flames, above the forest edge;
Flooding the silence in a silvern dream:
Conquering the night and all it's voices dumb,
With unheard melodies   While all agleam,
   Low flutes the lake along the lustrous sedge.

THE TIDES OF DAWN.

How cool across the lake's pearled, heaving floor,
  The spirit winds of morning steal in here:
  Dim mists of darkness rise from marsh and mere,
And pallid phantoms brood at morning's door.
Beyond yon east the surfs of dawning roar,
  To break in flame-waves on night's sombre beach;
  The heart still hears their impetuous, golden speech,
Imploring morn the daylight to restore.

Soon, soon, across the night's gray, ruined walls,
  Will flood and surge the crimson tides of morn;
  Bathing the east and all the dusks forlorn;
Soon, soon, across the dawn's white silence falls
  Glory and music, morning's song and fire:
  The waking world leaps to the day's desire.

CRAGS.*

Gaunt, huge, misshapen, 'neath the northern night,
  These wild lake crags loom black against the sky,
  While at their feet the restless waters sigh
And beat and moan amid the fitful light.
Here no life comes or takes it's shadowy flight,
  No voice save winds that shoreward faint and die;
  But ever through their weird rifts tow'ring high,
The moon with ray of gold the lake doth smite.

Men call them warrior-souls to adamant turned
Doomed through these thousand years that since have burned,
  To guard the prisoned souls that wander here;
So, dead to hate and waste, the centuries' storms,
True to their trust, they lift their awful forms,
  And keep these passes bleak, these regions drear.

*Among the Ojibway nations there is a legend that the lime-stone crag-cliffs on the shores of the great American lakes, are Indian warriors eternally fixed in stone by Nana Boza (Hiawatha) to keep guard over the spirits of bad Indians who are doomed to roam for ever these desolate wilds.

MEDWAYOSH.

A WORLD of dawn, where sky and water merge
In far, dim vapors, mingling blue in blue,
Where low-rimmed shores shimmer like gold shot
    through
Some misty fabric. Lost in dreams, I urge
With languid oar my skiff through sunny surge,
  That rings its music round the rocks and sands,
  Passing to silence, where far lying lands
Loom blue and purpling from the morning's verge.

I linger in dreams, and through my dreaming comes,
Like sound of suffering heard through battle drums,
  An anguished call of sad, heart-broken speech ;
As if some wild lake spirit, long ago,
Soul-wronged, through hundred years its wounded woe
  Moans out in vain across each wasted beach.

AT THE RIVER'S MOUTH.

A WORLD of mist and sky and watery waste
  Of windy reed-beds, where the river sifts
  Its silent waters, dreaming as it drifts
By hazy shores, unmindful of the haste
Of its old longing, when a wild wan life,.
  Panting for some dim future, it sped on,
  A gleaming ghost, far under dusk and dawn,
Stabbing the misty midnight, like a knife.

And now like one from maddened dream awake,
  Its wild, impetuous passion spent and old,
It threads a world of things that only seem ;
Mingling at last with its long-wished-for lake,
  Mid such a peace not even love foretold,
Where only dream-gods fold their wings and dream.

PART II.

SNOWFLAKES
AND
SUNBEAMS.

SNOW.

Down out of heaven,
  Frost-kissed
And wind driven,
  Flake upon flake,
  Over forest and lake,
Cometh the snow.

Folding the forest,
  Folding the farms,
In a mantle of white;
  And the river's great arms,
Kissed by the chill night
  From clamor to rest,
Lie all white and shrouded
  Upon the world's breast.

Falling so slowly
  Down from above,
So white, hushed, and holy,
  Folding the city

Like the great pity
  Of God in His love;
Sent down out of heaven
  On its sorrow and crime,
Blotting them, folding them
  Under its rime.

Fluttering, rustling,
  Soft as a breath,
The whisper of leaves,
  The low pinions of death,
Or the voice of the dawning,
  When day has its birth,
Is the music of silence
  It makes to the earth.

Thus down out of heaven,
  Frost-kissed
And wind-driven,
  Flake upon flake,
Over forest and lake,
  Cometh the snow.

CANADIAN FOLKSONG.

THE doors are shut, the windows fast;
Outside the gust is driving past,
Outside the shivering ivy clings,
While on the hob the kettle sings.
   Margery, Margery, make the tea,
   Singeth the kettle merrily.

The streams are hushed up where they flowed,
The ponds are frozen along the road,
The cattle are housed in shed and byre,
While singeth the kettle on the fire.
   Margery, Margery, make the tea,
   Singeth the kettle merrily.

The fisherman on the bay in his boat
Shivers and buttons up his coat;
The traveller stops at the tavern door,
And the kettle answers the chimney's roar.
   Margery, Margery, make the tea,
   Singeth the kettle merrily.

The firelight dances upon the wall,
Footsteps are heard in the outer hall;
A kiss and a welcome that fill the room,
And the kettle sings in the glimmer and gloom.
  Margery, Margery, make the tea,
  Singeth the kettle merrily.

TO A ROBIN IN NOVEMBER.

Sweet, sweet, and the soft listening heaven reels
In one blue ecstasy above thy song.
In the red heart of all the opening year,
In the hushed murmur of low dreaming fields
Hung under heaven 'twixt dim blue and blue;
Where the young Summer, purpled and pearled in
    dew,
Mirrors herself in June, and knows no wrong.

Sweet, sweet, throwing thy lack of fear
Back to the heart of God, till heaven feels
The throbbing of earth's music through and through.

Dreaming in song,— great pulsing-hearted hills,
Cradling the dawn in mists and purple veils
Of vapors, over pearls of lakes and brooks
Girdled about the neck of half the world,
When the red birth of the young dreaming June

To a Robin in November.

Kisses the lands with gales, and murmurs, and trills
Of melody, lips that blossom with tales
Of music and color and form and beauty of looks
And snowy argosies in heaven furled,
All summer set to one sweet, warbled tune.

And thou, red-throated, comest back to me
Here in the bare November bleak and chill,
Breathing the red-ripe of the lusty June
Over the rime of withered field and mere;
O heart of music, while I dream of thee,
Thou gladdest note in the dead Summer's tune,
Great God! thou liest dead outside my sill,
Starved of the last chill berry on thy tree,
Like some sweet instrument left all unstrung,
The melodious orchestra of all the year.
Dead with the sweet dead summer thou had'st sung;
Dead with the dead year's voices and clasp of hands;
Dead with all music and love and laughter and light;
While chilly and bleak comes up the winter night,
And shrieks the gust across the leafless lands.

IN THE STUDY.

OUT over my study,
All ashen and ruddy,
Sinks the December sun:
And high up over
The chimney's soot cover,
The winter night wind has begun.

Here in the red embers
I dream old Decembers,
Until the low moan of the blast,
Like a voice out of Ghost-land,
Or memory's lost-land,
Seems to conjure up wraiths from the past.

Then into the room
Through the firelight and gloom,
Some one steals, — let the night wind grow bleak,
And ever so coldly, —
Two white arms enfold me,
And a sweet face is close to my cheek.

ON CHRISTMAS EVE.

IN byre and barn the mows are brim with sheaves,
  Where stealeth in with phosphorescent tread
The glimmering moon, and, 'neath his wattled eaves,
The kennelled hound unto the darkness grieves
  His chilly straw, and from his gloom-lit shed,
  The wakeful cock proclaims the midnight dread.

With mullioned windows, 'mid its skeleton trees,
  Beneath the moon the ancient manor stands;
Old gables rattle in the midnight breeze,
Old elms make answer to the moaning seas
  Beyond the moorlands, on the wintry sands,
  While drives the gust along the leafless lands.

BY THE FIRE.

Hear the wind over the chimney,
  How it whistles and croons and sings,
And the flames and sparks fly upward,
  As if borne on unseen wings.

The moon like a silver crescent
  Peers under the elm-tree bough,
And the city of frost on the window pane
  Is illuminated now.

I cower and fancy and fancy,
  Till far in the middle night,
The hopes of a vanished past lie dead,
  Like the ashes dead and white.

LITTLE BLUE EYES AND GOLDEN HAIR.

LITTLE blue eyes and golden hair
Sits like a fairy beside my chair,
And gazes with owlish look on the fire,
Where the great log crackles upon his pyre;
And down in my heart there broods a prayer —
God bless blue eyes and golden hair.

Little blue eyes and golden hair
Chatters and laughs and knows no care;
Though far outside the night is bleak,
And under the eaves the shrill winds shriek
And rattle the elm boughs chill and bare —
God bless blue eyes and golden hair.

Little blue eyes and golden hair,
Taken all sudden and unaware,
Caught in the toils of the drowsy god,

Has gone on a trip to the Land of Nod;
Half fallen in my lap she lies,
With a warp of dreams in her lash-hid eyes;
And deep in my heart still broods that prayer—
God bless blue eyes and golden hair.

BARBERRIES.

BARBERRIES clustering on the bare walls,
 What is the beauty with which you glow?
 What are the blushes of secrets you know?
Flaming each spot where my footstep falls,
Barberries clustering on the bare walls.

Barberries clustering on the bare walls,
 I know two lips as red as your red;
 Two cheeks as blushing with love unsaid,
A heart whose glowing your glow recalls;
Barberries clustering on the bare walls.

Flame with it, flame with it, over your walls,
 Whisper my love of it, round the bleak year;
 'Till love makes summer of winter drear,
And heart holds heart in the sweetest of thralls;
Barberries clustering on the bare walls.

THE PASSING YEAR.

LIKE vikings came the rude blasts of November
   Chanting aloud the death song of the year;
Sadder and bleaker came the pale December,
With haggard woods and fitful dying ember,
   And leaves all dead and sere,
              Withered and sere.

I sit alone where the bright hearth-logs gleaming
   Into the gusty night red sparks do send;
The chimney's moan doth answer to my dreaming,
And the old year hath to me all the seeming
   Of a familiar friend,
              An old but vanished friend.

Bloweth the winter, from his forest leaping,
   Loud Boreas cometh from bleak arctic field,
Cometh with white gust in the midnight sweeping,
And findeth the Old Year like some Norse-king
      sleeping
   Upon his battle shield,
              With white locks, on his shield.

A WINTER'S NIGHT.

SHADOWY white,
Over the fields are the sleeping fences,
　Silent and still in the fading light,
As the wintry night commences.

The forest lies
On the edge of the heavens, bearded and brown;
　He pulls still closer his cloak, and sighs,
As the evening winds come down.

The snows are wound
As a winding sheet on the river's breast,
　And the shivering blast goes wailing round,
As a spirit that cannot rest.

Calm sleeping night!
Whose jewelled couch reflects the million stars
　That murmur silent music in their flight—
O, naught thy fair sleep mars.

A Winter's Night.

    And all a dream —
Thy spangled forest in its frosty sleep,
    Thy pallid moon that sheds its misty beam,
And looming wraiths that o'er the moorlands creep.

    As through the night
The trailing snows wind as a funeral train,
    And softly through the murky morning light
The dim grey day comes stealing up again.

OLD VOICES.

I STAND on the confines of the past to-night —
　The world that is gone before;
And in the dim flicker of the parlor light
Old shadows steal before my sight
　From its strange and misty shore.

And bygone murmurs are in my ears,
　And sweet lips touch my cheeks;
And old, old tunes, that no one hears,
Now steal to me from the sad old years,
　And sweet words that no one speaks.

But only the rythm of an old-time tune,
　That steals down the halls of time;
And comes so soft, like the far-off rune
Of a stream that sleeps through the afternoon,
　Or a distant evening chime.

And in the silence that intervenes
  Sad voices whisper low;
Come back once more to the loved old scenes —
To the dim old region of boyhood's dreams —
  To the sweet world you used to know.

FEBRUARY.

Thou chilly month of wind and rain,
Of drifting at the whited pane,
'Twixt winter's birth and winter's wane;

Thou shrouded month of muffled snows,
Of gales from far-off arctic floes,
When winter dieth of his woes;

Dost thou not through thine ice-bound girth,
Hear, in the warmer heart of earth,
The young spring dreaming of its birth,

When, stealing through thy mailéd, strong
Ice-armor, comes the sweet low song
Of pied wind flowers, their streams along,

With sweet first-thoughts and prophesies
Of warm, wet winds and soft, blue skies
And meadows all a green surprise?

O, go thy way with gust and blow, —
For all thy looks of wintry woe,
Thou had'st a warm heart 'neath thy snow.

And all thy bluster and thy gust
A softer nature did encrust,
Which had the whole year's hopes in trust.

MIDWINTER NIGHT'S DREAM.

THE snows outside are white and white,
The gusty flue shouts through the night,
And by the lonely chimney light
    I sit and dream of summer.

The orchard bough creaks in the blast,
That like a ghost goes shrieking past,
And coals are dying fast and fast,
    But still I dream of summer.

'Tis not the voice of falling rain,
Or dream wind blown through latticed pane,
When earth will laugh in green again,
    That makes me dream of summer.

But hopes will then have backward flown,
Like fleets of promise long out-blown,
And Love once more will greet his own,—
    This is my dream of summer.

ON A MARCH MORNING.

OUR elm is heavy with ice,
The mountain is hid in a mist,
  And the heaven is grey
  Above, and away,
Where the vapors the hill-tops have kissed.

The fields are bleak patches of white,
Our stream is still shut in his prison
  Of ice and of snow,
  And the sun, half-aglow,
Scarce over the forest is risen.

But there is something abroad in the air,
Perchance 'tis the spirit of spring,
  That fills me with fancies
  Of blue skies and pansies,
And songs that the meadow brooks sing.

Some spirit the season has sent,
With visions of blossom and leaf,
And song—as a token,
Of feeling unspoken,
In this time of the aged winter's grief.

SUNBEAMS.

They weave a web of light and shade
　In leafy nooks at noon,
And in the caverns of night they spin
　The white locks of the moon.

They build the walls of nature's house,
　Each smites with a golden bar;
They climb down at night on silver strands,
　And each is tied to a star;

And then at dawn they softly steal
　In the east, through their golden door,
And weave a woof of roseate hues
　On the ocean's shimmering floor.

And every pearl of lustrous tint,
　And every gem divine,
That borrows its light from the ocean's night,
　Is the child of their airy mine.

And whether by night or whether by day
They loosen their shining skein,
It falls down out of the heaven's deep
In a silver or golden rain.

BEFORE THE DAWN.

ONE hour before the flush of dawn,
　That all the rosy daylight weaves,
Here in my bed, far overhead
　I hear the swallows in the eaves.

I cannot see, but well I know,
　That out around the dusky grey,
Across dark lakes and voicéd streams,
　The blind, dumb vapors feel their way.

And here and there a star looks down
　Out of the fog that holds the sea
In its embrace, while up the lands,
　Some cock makes music lustily.

And out within the dreamy woods,
　Or in some clover blossomed lawn,
The blinking robin pipes his mate
　To wake the music of the dawn.

THE DEWDROP.

I FELL from heaven at golden dawn
  Like a tear from the sky's blue deep;
I fell in the cell of a lily's bell,
  And woke all the world from sleep.

The cock called out from his drowsy shed,
  The humming-bee woke to his feast,
And sleep blew off from the eyes of men,
  As the mists blew out of the east.

Phœbus harnessed his snorting steeds,
  And let down his golden bars,
And strewed the fields of heaven with red,
  As the night blew out with the stars.

Then Helios rose from his streams in the east,
  And smote on the doors of day,
And the worker arose from his rest to toil,
  And the priest in his cell to pray.

INDIAN SUMMER.

Along the line of smoky hills
  The crimson forest stands,
And all the day the blue-jay calls
  Throughout the autumn lands.

Now by the brook the maple leans
  With all his glory spread,
And all the sumachs on the hills
  Have turned their green to red.

Now by great marshes wrapt in mist,
  Or past some river's mouth,
Throughout the long, still autumn day
  Wild birds are flying south.

TO A CLUMP OF MOSS.

Low thou sleepest, where the wood is deepest,
　　Green and cool,
In the great shady gloom of the wood,
　　Beside some pool.

To thee is given the dew of heaven
　　Alone to drink,
Out of the crystal flagons the night
　　Lets down from the heaven's brink.

RODODACTULOS.

THE night blows outward in a mist,
And all the world the sun has kissed.

Along the golden rim of sky,
A thousand snow-piled vapors lie.

And by the wood and mist-clad stream,
The Maiden Morn stands still to dream.

THE MEADOW SPRING.

HERE, in a deep, blue cavern of the sun,
  Like some lost jewel, in the tangled grass
    I lie, where cloudlets ever pass and pass,
And o'er my breast the unseen breezes run.
Deep in my crystal heart, fallen one by one
  From out the burnished quiver of the sky,
    The sunbeams' golden shafted arrows lie.
O, dreamer of the summer lands, but come,
  And, bending down, gaze on my silent face,
When from the sky's high dome all clouds are furled.
  And I will show you, by the season's grace,
    What I by subtlest charm have conjured here —
    A universe of beauty in a tear —
A mirrored glimpse of all the glowing world.

PART III.
OTHER POEMS.

LAZARUS.

O, Father Abram, I can never rest,
  Here in thy bosom in the whitest heaven,
  Where love blooms on through days without an even;
  For up through all the paradises seven,
There comes a cry from some fierce, anguished breast.

A cry that comes from out of hell's dark night,
  A piercing cry of one in agony,
  That reaches me here in heaven white and high;
  A call of anguish that doth never die;
Like dream-waked infant wailing for the light.

O, Father Abram, heaven is love and peace,
  And God is good; eternity is rest.
  Sweet would it be to lie upon thy breast
  And know no thought but loving to be blest
Save for that cry that never more will cease.

It comes to me above the angel-lyres,
The chanting praises of the cherubim ;
It comes between my upward gaze and Him,
All-blessed Christ. A voice from the vague dim,
"*O, Lazarus, come and ease me of these fires.*"

"*O, Lazarus, I have called thee all these years,
It is so long for me to reach to thee,
Across the ages of this mighty sea,
That loometh dark, dense, like eternity ;
Which I have bridged by anguished prayers and
tears.*

"*Which I have bridged by knowledge of God's love,
That even penetrates this anguished glare ;
A gleaming ray, a tremulous, star-built stair,
A road by which love-hungered souls may fare
Past hate and doubt, to heaven and God above.*"

So calleth it ever upward unto me.
It creepeth in through heaven's golden doors,

It echoes all along the saphire floors,
Like smoke of sacrifice, it soars and soars,
It fills the vastness of eternity.

Until my sense of love is waned and dimmed,
  The music-rounded spheres do clash and jar,
  No more those spirit-calls from star to star,
  The harmonies that float and melt afar,
The belts of light by which all heaven is rimmed.

No more I hear the beat of heavenly wings,
  The seraph chanting in my rest-tuned ear;
  I only know a cry, a prayer, a tear,
  That rises from the depths up to me here;
A soul that to me suppliant leans and clings.

O, Father Abram, thou must bid me go
  Into the spaces of the deep abyss;
  Where far from us and our God-given bliss,
  Do dwell those souls that have done Christ amiss;
For through my rest I hear that upward wo.

I hear it crying through the heavenly night,
  When curvéd, hung in space, the million moons
  Lean planet-ward, and infinite space attunes
  Itself to silence, as from drear gray dunes,
A cry is heard along the shuddering light,

Of wild dusk-bird, a sad, heart-curd'ling cry,
  So comes to me that call from out hell's coasts;
  I see an infinite shore with gaping ghosts;
  This is no heaven, with all it's shining hosts;
This is no heaven until that hell doth die.

So spake the soul of Lazarus, and from thence,
  Like new-fledged bird from its sun-jewelled nest,
  Drunk with the music of the young year's quest;
  He sank out into heaven's gloried breast,
Spaceward turned, toward darkness dim, immense.

Hellward he moved like radiant star shot out
  From heaven's blue with rain of gold at even',
  When Orion's train and that mysterious seven

Move on in mystic range from heaven to heaven.
Hellward he sank, followed by radiant rout.

The liquid floor of heaven bore him up,
   With unseen arms, as in his feathery flight,
   He floated down toward the infinite night;
   But each way downward, on the left and right,
He saw each moon of heaven like a cup

Of liquid, misty fire that shone afar
   From sentinel towers of heaven's battlements;
   But onward, winged by love's desire intense,
   And sank, space-swallowed, into the immense.
While with him ever widened heaven's bar.

'Tis ages now long-gone since he went out,
   Christ-urged, love-driven, across the jasper walls,
   But hellward still he ever floats and falls,
   And ever nearer come those anguished calls;
And far behind he hears a glorious shout.

THE HEBREW FATHER'S PRAYER.

O THOU, just One, who givest gifts to men,
 Who holdest light and darkness in thy hand,
 Who alone can blight and bless, whose strong
  command
Can make a garden of a darksome fen:
 O Thou who lovest all and hatest none,
  Look down, compassionate, I pray, on me.
 Not for myself but for the sake of one,
  The little child that smileth at my knee.

Men say we come of a dark, cursed race,
 Who fell in bitterness from out thy word,
 Who slew Thy blessed Son — a ruthless horde —
And gave Him gall to drink, and smote His face:
 O Thou who knowest all, let not this blight,
  This awful blight come down; but if it be,
 Send it on my dark life, not her's so bright,
  The little child that smileth at my knee.

The Hebrew Father's Prayer.

Thou knowest I have sinned and fallen short
  Of all thy laws, that I was reared in hate
  And bitterness as dread as their's who wait,
In gloom and darkness round hell's baleful court.
  But pity, Lord, O pity my distress,
    Let all thy righteous sentence fall on me,
  Consume me utterly, if Thou wilt bless
    The little child that smileth at my knee.

O take me, Lord, and make me what Thou wilt,
  Give me to drink whole centuries of wo,
  For her dear sake who is as driven snow,
Plunge agony's cruel sword clean to the hilt:
  Heap on me all, O what would I not bear:
    For deepest hell were heaven indeed to me,
  To know that thou didst have her in thy care,
    The little child that smileth at my knee.

Then spake God's angel, answering thus, "Old man,
  Thy love so white hath burnt out all thy sin,
  Where thy child goes thou too shalt enter in,
Heaven hath no hate for thee in all it's plan.

God made love strong that it might whiten all,
Might conquer all, and make all thereby free.
Thou lovest thy God in loving that one small,
Unconscious child that smileth at thy knee.

ODE TO TENNYSON.

GREAT Bard, thou Merlin of these latter days,
Who wovest thy magic songs in looms of thought,
From out the dim threads of the misty past;
Sweetest and strongest in song since Milton sang,
Or Shakespeare by his Avon dreamed of Lear;
Thine Arthur with his helm of gleaming light,
Hath sent a wind of thought about the world;
A glory like the glory of the Grail,
To lead men higher to our Lord Divine.

To thee, great agéd, round the shining world,
Across Atlantic and his fogs and gloom,
And gleaming breast — a mirror of moon and stars,
And dawns and sunsets, when the ruddy sun
Drives, flaming, his fiery car from east to west,
Across the vapors of the upper deep,
I pay this humble tribute to thy song,

My master, nor I shame to call thee so,
But rather glory to have drunk from thee,

And thy deep springs of song, as Virgil did,
Greater than I, from that old Grecian bard
Who sang in dark, immortal songs for men.
As here upon our western continent,
The great St. Lawrence, all night long, flows north
Into the mighty waters of his gulf,
And sings a glorious song to all his shores,
Caught by the dawn and breathed across the world;
So sang he mighty songs, great songs of light,
That streamed through all the caverns of his thought,
And brimmed the mighty rivers of his brain.

Or Milton, blind, the bard of newer days,
The glorious Homer of our own loved tongue,
Who sang in lofty strains of heavenly wars,
Of light and dark, when heaven and hell arrayed
Against each other, Satan downward fell,
A baleful star, with constellation dire,
Into the dread abysses of the deep.
Or sang he sweeter musiced-pastoral lays,
Like him of Mantua, sweet-voiced Roman bard,
Who sang of sylvan woods and breezy farms;

Great shady beeches where some shepherd piped
His amorous strains amid his fleecy flocks.

O father poet, let me call thee so,
I, thy disciple, sitting at thy feet,
Thou master of song in all its varied chords,
Bird lyrist of the music of our time,
Had I thy voice, or his, our own loved dead,
Who here by winding Charles 'neath western skies,
Like John on Patmos, saw the inner light,
And breathed to men the music of his dream;
Thou like the eagle, he the soaring lark,
Thy brother bard in song, cleaving the air,
So near to heaven heard the angels sing
And brought some echo back, down here to men.
Had I his voice or thine I would aspire,
As birds attempt to cleave the edge of clouds,
Away above them in the upper air;
To be a voice to thee, a nameless voice,
Voice of the new west calling to the east,
To tell thee of this wondrous western world;
Voice of the future calling to the past,

O'er silent lakes and rivers round the world,
To where thou dwellest in thy English halls,
With mighty ruins of the ivied past,
With all its chronicles of wars and kings
And greater, for the web of all the past
Is wove in mystic colors, we may take
And many of these patterns make our own;
And so make strong the future from the past.

Great bard, thou ever seemest unto me,
In all the broils and turmoils of the state;
Like some aged Lear of truth and holy light,
Wandering amid a wreck of men and kings
And broken swords of honor,—worn out creeds,
And all the vanished dream of England's past.
A voice of anguish for the trampled right,
A voice of warning for the future good;
That goes so like a breath of midnight wind,
Blown through a lonely haunted place of tombs.
And there thou walkest, white-haired, aged, bent,
About the night of life, with one vain call,

Heard 'mid the turmoil of the lower world,
For some Cordelia of the purer past.

And more, for thou art also unto me
Like some lost knight of the great order gone;
Sir Bedivere last of the table round,
Or Arthur himself, dying of all his wounds,
Not wounds of flesh alone, but wounds of sins,
Wounds of the heart for those who were untrue.
So the old order goes, last baron great
Of England's greatness, states dissolve and wane
And governments decline, old customs die;
But memory in men is never dead,
And character and greatness all remain,
Like stars set in the firmament of time,
To shine for all days on. A star thou art
Of greatest magnitude and from thy light,
Thou too shalt build a ring of lesser lights,
To burn forever in thy radiance,
Reflecting all thy glory to the world.

ODE.

CANADA TO GREAT BRITAIN.
(1887.)

GREAT mother of nations, whose hand
  Holds half the world's sway in its grasp;
With commerce's shimmering band
  Encircling all earth in thy clasp.

Thou breaker of fetters and thralls,
  Thou maker of wars and of peace;
The mighty sea waves for thy walls,
  The people of earth thine increase.

The shock of the ages unfelt,
  Thou brood of the Saxon and Dane;
Unmoved while old monarchies melt,
  Still strong while the centuries wane.

From the land of the north and the west,
  From the land of the maple and pine;
O'er Atlantic's broad billowy breast,
  To the tribute of song, I add mine.

To the surging of voice and of heart,
  Over mountain, plain, ocean and sea;
Where half the wide earth hath her part,
  In rendering of tribute to thee.

Outblown by each favoring wind,
  Thy war-bristling armaments toss;
Thou guardian of either far Ind.,
  Defender of Crescent and Cross.

Beneath the broad wing of thy sway,
  All creeds, tongues and nations keep tryst;
Greece, Araby, Egypt, Cathay,
  Mohammed, Brahm, Budda, and CHRIST.

Thou wielder of strength tested long,
  Thou builder of days yet to be;
The strong and the weak and the strong,
  The future and past, meet in thee.

Not built was thy power in a day,
  Not a sudden upheaval thy might;

But slowly, like dawn's brightening ray,
It grew from the centuries' night.

But thou, beloved, honored and great,
Who hast so much good in thy power;
Earth's Lazarus lies at thy gate,
O pass him not by; 'tis thine hour!

With the torch of the age in thy hands,
God given — then be it Christ-spent;
From all continents, nations, all lands,
Are truth-seeking eyes on thee bent.

Go give them the light that they want,
Go teach them what God hath taught thee:
Not lies, hatred, meanness, and cant,
But the knowledge that maketh all free.

And more, by the gifts of thy past,
By thine unswerving trust in thy God;
To the winds all old tyrannies cast,
Lay down the old sceptre of blood.

Take up the new sceptre of peace,
  Show mightier deeds can be done,
In wisdom, and battles surcease,
  Than Agincourt, Waterloo won.

Old bitterness, sorrow and wrong,
  The centuries' murmur and groan;
Cannot be forgot, like a song,
  In the smoke of a cannon out-blown.

Show the dark age of serfdom is past,
  Show the better, the stronger, the true
Where freedom bright halo will cast
  On old truths that forever are new.

Where sciences' blindlings may grope,
  In the gleam of faith's uprisen sun;
Where a common sweet freedom and hope,
  Will weld all thy peoples in one.

ODE TO THE NINETEENTH CENTURY.

DIM dawn of a nobler future, late night of a holier past;
Twilight of truth's torches wasted, bread on the waters long cast;
Time long weary of gleaning old husks from the fields that are bleak,
Age dead to the oracles uttered, and the droning of lips that still speak.
Age of little that's earnest, age of nothing that's strong,
Age of wills that are broken, true to no passion long;
With the dregs of a cup for a draught, and a feeble complaint for a song.
Small lakes where once was an ocean, little stars where once was a sun;
Wheels in confusion of wheels, where once the great circle was one.

What are our dreams of the future, what have we
  left of the past?
What are we dreaming or doing, how shall we
  meet the next blast?
Politics, politics, politics : ruin, confusion and rout,
In, chicanery, lying, model reformers when out.
Loud-mouthed babblings of honour, pratings of
  victories won,
Maggots that crawl in the foulness of a carcass out
  under the sun!

Modern civilization, widening; what doth it mean?
Better a healthy barbarism, than this last age hath
  been ;
With its social and moral lepers, crying; unclean!
  unclean !
Empires, monarchies, states ; all are one of a kind ;
Strife of atoms with atoms, blind ones leading the
  blind.
Little is anchored on justice, little is honest or wise ;
Passions buffeting passions, 'till God shall open
  their eyes.

Each hath a grain of knowledge, each hath a spark
of truth,
Hidden in dark and confusion, buried in ruin and
ruth.

Parties and sects and parties; despots, the curse of
the earth;
Chaining up knowledge and reason, crippling children
at birth.
Wide is the wisdom of God, wide as the bounds
of the world,
Would ye take it and hide it under a napkin
furled.

Petty, weak dreams of an hour, puerile reforms of a
week;
Are there not plans and plans outside the ends ye
seek?
Ye, who seek to compass the deeds of all time in
a day,
Ye, who trust in yourselves, scorning to wait or to
pray;

Are there not suns and suns where yours are
    dimmed in the grey?
Ye who take one plot out of the gardens of God,
Hedge it about with a creed, and water and tend
    its sod.
Are there not flowers and flowers that blossom
    outside of your ken?
Are there not seeds wide sown thick as the
    thoughts of men?
Think not yours are all under the breadth of the
    blue,
There are flowers as *fair* just as holy of hue.

ODE TO A MEADOW BROOK.

DREAM on, dream on, enamoured of thy lot,
  Thou child of summer 'mid thy fields and trees,
Where haply in some low, wind-cradled spot,
  Red, sunbeam-kissed, and garnered sweet of bees,
Bright clovers nod, loved by each languid breeze.
  Dream on, dream on, by gables, nooks and farms,
Where gladness smiles and beauty never flees,
  Outside of all that hates and all that harms,
Unmindful of our life and its vague weak alarms.

Dream on, dream on, 'neath gentle skies low furled,
  By soft tongued airs and honied blossoms blest,
Across the bosom of the under world,
  Where sunbeams kiss through its green throbbing vest.
Thou art a part of nature, on her breast,
  A prattling infant thou wilt ever lie,

Drawing all music from her mighty rest,
  Sweet melodies though old yet never die,
  But mingle their glad dream with wood and field and sky.

Dream on, dream on, and tell all time thy love;
  Of earth and all her misty, leafy dress,
Of sun and moon and stars, blue heaven above,
  Too tranced in love's sweet self-forgetfulness,
To dream how much thine own glad life doth bless
  All things in meadow, marsh and leafy wold.
Nor maketh thus its own glad music less,
  (Like human love that waneth wan and cold)
  But folds and clasps all else in its sweet shining fold.

ALONE.

HERE in the night I sit alone,
　Where far above the aged roof,
Half mossed, and half with vines o'er-grown,
　The starlight weaves a silver woof,
And falls in flakes where all unknown,
Out in the night I sit alone.

Here all alone where only comes
　The moon's white feet before the dawn,
I sit and list the dreary hums
　Of night sounds where all life is gone,
While night its lonely cycle sums,
And wait a *step* that never comes.

'Tis only for a ghost I wait,
　The wraith of something gone before,
Some past, some sweet, long-dreamed-of state,
　Whose memory is my only store;
Like Lazarus at the rich man's gate,
Here 'neath the stars I watch and wait.

Alone.

I watch and wait, but never comes
    The voice I long had loved to hear,
Through weary hours the cricket hums
    Weird music, and the night is drear,
And while its lonely cycle sums,
I wait a step that never comes.

BALLADE OF TWO RIDERS.

GALLOPING, galloping, galloping, over the sunset world,
Out of the past and its strife into the future hurled,
Out of the past and its cry into the misty to-be,
Two riders gallop alone, out to the northland sea.
Far from the dunes behind cometh the world's vain call,
But these two gallop alone past the shadows that fall,
Into a region of mists that far to the northward lies;
Her world but the dream of his face, his sun but the light of her eyes.

"O love, to gallop alone, out here in this weird, wild land,
Where the winds of remembrance blow not over the shifting sand;
Where the deeds that are done are dead, and the past lies buried behind;

With hate that is cruel and strong, and fate that is
  crippled and blind.
Never to know again the scoff and the wounding
  jest,
The voice of morning that wakens the pang in the
  sorrowful breast;
But loved face dreaming on loved face, into the
  misty to-be,
Galloping, galloping, galloping, out to the northward
  sea."

What doth she see in his face? What is it he
  readeth in hers?
Speed like the wind their chargers, needing nor
  whip nor spurs.
"O love, lean nearer, lean nearer:" in vain dead
  phantoms arise.
"O love, draw closer, draw closer:" he drinks but
  the light of her eyes.
Far over the dunes and the dusk-lands, the murmur
  of human life

Ballade of Two Riders.

Goes up from the strong and the weary, the old
    and the young in the strife;
The cry of the broken-hearted, the sob of the
    vanquished ones,
The dim, far curfew and matins of dying and waking
    suns,
But dead to the surge and the tumult, visage loved
    visage upon,
Wrapt in their love, these lovers for ever and ever
    ride on.

Galloping, galloping, galloping, knowing not morning
    or noon,
Only escaped to the night out of the dim afternoon;
Like wraiths of themselves that are dead, into the
    dusk and the mist,
Galloping, galloping, galloping, shadow and sunbeam
    kissed.
Face on face illumined, set to the seaward sun,
Galloping, galloping, galloping, ride these two lovers
    as one.

What are the sights and the sounds unto their eyes and their ears?
What is the world with its woes, its doubts, its cares and its fears?
Battle and battle's surcease, silence and thunder of gun
May startle the world, but deaf they ride to the seaward sun.
"O love, lean nearer, lean nearer;" the days of the past are dead,
"O love, draw closer, draw closer;" the even forever is red.

A LYRIC OF LOVE.

Up out of the lower abysms, the regions of woe,
Sprang, flame-like, a voice, from the pit fires that lower and glow.

O, soul of my soul, thou purest, thou heavenly one,
Sin-bound to this flame through the ages my being was run.

Till out of the gates of the morning thou camest afar,
Down here to the dusk and the moan, like the the flight of a star.

Thou camest adown through the ether from morning and bliss,
To find me, and cool my parched spirit with kiss upon kiss.

For love were not love that could die, being planted in thee,

A Lyric of Love.

Not God nor the angels in heaven could keep thee from me.

The creatures of burning did taunt me through ages of night,
Till thou camest down here and withered them all with thy light.

Till wasting like sea gnomes at clangor of dawn-waking bell,
They shuddering fled to the confines of nethermost hell.

Thy white arms about me, were cooling like driftings of snow.
Thine eyes on mine eyes like seas on volcanoes below.

Thy soul healed the woe of my soul through the ages of hours,
Thy lips on my lips like the dewy sweet freshness of flowers.

Till hell were no longer a hell, but a heaven below,
O love, with the strength of thy love thou slewest my woe.

Thou slewest my hate of God and the angels above,
And sprouted a germ that blossomed, O love, into love.

Thou didst 'lumine the darkness, and through the long nights of the years,
Thou didst quench out the flame from my heart with the rain of thy tears.

Till with clinking of chain upon chain, loosed the manacled fires,
That prisoned my spirit in fetters of demon desires.

They loosen! those hell-bonds, from off me, like falling of clod,
O, hide me, pure love, in thy soul, thou takest me back to my God.

THE PHANTOMS OF THE BOUGHS ON THE WINDOW.

I sit before my fire in the waning April light,
Where like an awful genie comes the shadow of the night.
Outside the naked elms moan the vanished season's grief,
And a windy, pallid flicker throws in ghastly, dim relief,
The phantoms of the boughs on the window.

To the fire I draw my chair, but I know that they are there,
Those terrible, wan ghosts of the dead, gone year's despair.
And I try to dream of hope, but my heart can only grope,
In the darkness, like a drowning man who clutches for a rope,
With those phantoms of the boughs on my window.

152 *The Phantoms of the Boughs on the Window.*

For they seem so like the ghosts of my own departed dreams,
Where the skeleton remains of the life that only seems:
For they also nestled blossoms, and the birds sang on each bough,
And the sunbeams wove each girdle, but what remaineth now
But the phantoms of the boughs on the window?

So I had my summer's youth, when I dreamed life was a truth,
And I dared with laughing lips the approach of fate and ruth:
But the visions are all fled, with the skies no longer red,
And I bow my lonely head, for my genius it is dead,
Like the phantoms of the boughs on the window.

The summer comes again, and the music of the rain,

Will warm the elms back to the life that they
 would fain:
And the robins they will sing, where the cool, green
 banners fling,
But to me no joys will wing, but the dead boughs
 only cling,
Like the phantoms of the boughs at the window.

And I know if one were dead, on the lonely cham-
 ber bed,
And a sad soul were divorcèd from the sorrow that
 men wed:
If a heart were still and silent from the fretting and
 the care:
I know they would be there, as if mocking mute
 despair,
The phantoms of the boughs on the window.

TITAN.

TITAN — he loves a breezy hill
 Away above us in the clouds,
Where sun and wind are never still,
 And fold it round with misty shrouds.

He loves the great world stretching out
 Into dim sky; he loves the flowers
And trees, the brooks that laugh and shout,
 And often he will sit for hours

And gaze into the distant rim
 Of all things made of earth and air,
That rounds the horizon vague and dim,
 Until his great, deep eyes do wear

A look of awe, in thoughts of One,
 Invisible, Eternal, Great,
Who built from out the burning sun,
 This glorious world with all its state.

And through the clouds, that like a crown
 Of snow encircle his hill's great head,

Sometimes the sun in peering down
    Will find him sleeping on his bed

Of clover lawn, with blossoms that strew
    Themselves like love, and round him wave,
And all the night the winds blow through
    His dreams as through a cave.

Brawny, huge-limbed, in frame and mind
    True type of man, in heart a boy,
Who loves the music of the wind,
    Who yet is innocent in joy.

Whose heart is not a cavern of doubt
    And dark foul hates, with passions rife;
His dreams are all of flowers about,
    His life is part of nature's life.

Though great in strength of manly form,
    His heart is truest tenderness,
Strong as the spirit of the storm,
    Soft as the rain drops when they press,

With cooling lips the parchéd flowers
  That peer like young birds from their nest,
Mouths gaping for the much-loved showers,
  That cool and nourish Nature's breast.

And there I know he sits at dawn
  Fresh from his cave of sleep, with eyes
Clear as the sky above, the lawn
  Resplendent with a thousand dyes.

A line of red that lights the east
  And widens over sky and sea
In purple and gold, and snowy fleeced,
  Where mountain peaks loom high and free.

And when pale May with tears the earth
  Has watered, and the rosier June
To balm and bloom has given birth,
  And strung the world to rarest tune,

Then I shall hie to Titan's hill
  Where far above among the clouds

The sun and wind are never still,
  But fold it round with misty shrouds.

And there 'mid lawns and grassy nooks,
  The great world stretching far below,
Here, far from men and care and books,
  Where only streams of nature flow.

And he shall teach me, he who drinks
  Where nature's fountains brimming run,
Who forged in thought the burning links
  That bind the great zones of the sun.

Whose nightly torches are the stars
  That look with ever-trusting eyes
Across the midnight's gloomy bars,
  And he will make me strong and wise.

ISOLATION.

To be alone, O God, to be alone,
  And never know the touch of kindly hand;
  Like some lone tree far out on barren sand
Where only nights and desert winds make moan,
Whence love and light and sympathy are flown;
  To be like riven pine on blasted land,
  To take no part in all earth's struggling band,
To be alone, O God, to be alone.

To never know the common lot or part,
To hold no place in any human heart,
  To pluck no flowers where love's wide bloom
    is sown —
If there be hell, 'tis isolation drear,
To never know a kiss, a sob, a tear;
To be alone, O God, to be alone.

INFANCY.

Weak, helpless wanderer from an unknown shore,
  Frail infant bark, but lately set adrift
  On life's rough waves, beneath it's angry lift.
To dare its strife, and meet its tempest roar,
Thy very weakness were thy richest store.
  Thou puny tyrant, love's own gladdest gift,
  Thou blossom fallen down the world's blue rift,
How thou dost coil about the heart's deep core.

O crowing lips and dimpled, clinging hands,
  Clear, laughing eyes and chubby, baby face,
  This world without thee were an empty place.
Thou makest paradise of all earth's lands,
  And bring'st a boon no other joys can grant,
  Thou latest bond in love's sweet covenant.

KNOWLEDGE.

WE are so quick to teach, so slow to learn,
  And life is such a strange, mysterious school,
  Wherein the soul hath neither law nor rule,
Save intuitions from the heart, that burn
And scathe the spirit, restless to discern
    That which is weak, and what is wholly strong,
    What lifteth up and beareth all along —
The one great law on which all lives do turn.

Go on dull spirit, tread thy purblind path,
  And nature, loving all, and hating none,
  Who grope in blindness toward the eternal sun,
In some far-distant human aftermath,
  The struggle done, and darkness over-past,
  Will give thee peace in knowledge at the last.

www.ingramcontent.com/pod-product-compliance
Lightning Source LLC
Chambersburg PA
CBHW031456160426
43195CB00010BB/1003